The Turbulent Life Of Healing

Tina M. Swoffer

First Paper Edition January 2025

Book Designed and Mapped By Tina M Swoffer.

DEDICATION

For years I said that each of my children taught me something I didn't yet know I needed.

Samantha taught me courage, the kind that rises in the moments when protection is the only choice.

Isaac taught me strength, how to walk away when necessary and keep us safe, even when it hurts.

Zavier taught me trust, through the obstacles we faced, both in his youth and adulthood, side by side.

Hunter taught me joy, how to laugh again and let the lighter parts of life fill my heart.

Kylee taught me individuality and softness—reminding me that gentleness is just as necessary as resilience.

Dalton taught me unconditional love and prophetic truth—the words I was once too afraid to share with the world.

And Bailey taught me forgiveness—the kind that returns again and again until you finally learn to embrace it.

Thank you, my children, for shaping me into the woman I am, not just as a mother, daughter, or friend, but as me, myself, and I.

You are each a chapter in my healing, and together, the story of my becoming.

Acknowledgments

This book was born from some of the hardest and most transformative seasons of my life, and I would not have reached this point without the people who walked with me, whether for a moment, a chapter, or the full journey.

To my seven incredible children and all my grandchildren, you are my heartbeat, my reason, and my reminder that love is always worth fighting for. Your strength and patience gave me room to grow, and your belief in me helped me believe in myself. You are forever the fuel to my fire.

To my family, friends, and the beautiful souls who stood beside me during moments of turbulence, thank you for holding space for my healing. Your presence, honesty, and compassion helped me rise when I could have stayed down.

To every mentor who offered guidance, tools, and wisdom. You helped me find my voice and rebuild the parts of me I thought were lost.

To the readers who pick up this book, thank you for trusting me with your own journey. My hope is that these words remind you that you're not alone and that healing, though messy, is powerful and possible.

And most of all, I thank God for the strength to keep going, for the clarity to turn pain into purpose, and for the calling to help others find their way back to themselves.

This book is for every person learning to and choosing to live 2 live!

The Turbulent Life of Healing: A Journey Through Chaos to Clarity

Life is rarely a smooth path. It's full of twists, turns, and moments that can leave us questioning our purpose, our worth, and our ability to keep moving forward. *The Turbulent Life of Healing* dives into the messy, unpredictable, and transformative journey of reclaiming your life after trauma, loss, and self-doubt.

Through candid storytelling and raw honesty, the author shares her experiences navigating a life marked by challenges and setbacks, yet fueled by resilience, courage, and a longing for something greater. This book is not just about overcoming hardship—it's about learning to thrive amidst it.

With heartfelt insights and practical tools, readers will discover the importance of embracing imperfection, setting boundaries, and cultivating self-love. From grappling with the pain of the past to rediscovering joy in the present, this book is a roadmap for anyone seeking to heal while living through life's storms.

Perfect for those yearning for hope and inspiration, *The Turbulent Life of Healing* is a reminder that even in the chaos, there is beauty, growth, and the possibility of a brighter tomorrow. This is your guide to finding clarity, peace, and purpose, no matter how turbulent the journey.

INTRODUCTION

Hello, my name is Tina M. Swoffer. I am a soon-to-be 50-year-old woman, a mother to 7 amazing children, and a "Gigi" to my grandchild. I became a widow at a young age—around 7 years ago, when I lost my best friend, pain-in-the-ass, father to our children, and husband. Yes, this is all one person.

Even before meeting my husband, my childhood was filled with turbulent lessons that have shaped who I am today. I've used those experiences to protect others and offer unconditional love.

Currently, I don't have a relationship with my biological mother, but I've been blessed with a plethora of wonderful women mentors who have shown me the life I desired or, in some cases, what I never wanted to experience or do to others. In my life so far, I've had moments where I stumbled into complacency and sacrificed my own hope for something better, for the sake of others' wants and needs.

At 18, I went to Al-Anon to understand my need for acceptance and love from my mother. I came to realize that she loved me the best way she knew how, and for that, I have always had hope and faith that there had to be more. Over the years, I had friends, families, grandparents, and aunts all trying their best to tame the wild heart I had as a child. But deep down, I was just screaming for validation and claim. Unfortunately, I received more attention when I was "smelling like shit" than when I was "smelling like honey," mostly because I had little to no self-love, value, or worth.

My father was the Marlboro man and, in his own way, wished he could fight for me. But back in those days, men didn't have much of a voice in raising kids. Despite this, I was fortunate to have amazing mentors in my grandparents and uncles. As a child, I observed everything around me.

Through my life experiences, I've worked hard to focus on the truth, and I'm thankful to my parents for teaching me everything they did, just by being who they were. I've taken those lessons and remembered how it felt to be treated in ways I didn't want others to experience. I'm not perfect— I'm sure I've hurt people along the way, and for that, I am truly sorry. But I also understand that the turbulence of life offers lessons that can lead to growth. These lessons will provide a deeper understanding of how to act in the world, knowing that these teachings will come into play again, perhaps not until you're 50, but they will.

Becoming a mother changed everything for me. The unconditional love of a child opened my heart and mind to learning more about what each child would bring to the world. My oldest gave me courage, the next brought strength, another showed me sympathy, another taught me balance, one shared humor, another taught me karma, and the last one shared wisdom. Now that my grandkids are here, I see and feel that the idea of legacy is much bigger and more powerful than I ever imagined.

Many times, I wonder how a parent can just let go or not want to be part of their child's life. But for me, perhaps not having that relationship with my biological mother was a blessing in disguise. As I became a mother, wife, and widow, navigating multiple jobs and businesses, I realized that there is really nothing you can't do—you're only restricted by saying "can't" or refusing to try. Going through the hardest paths and making tough choices doesn't make you bad; the hope is that it makes you stronger, helping you fight harder and longer for the most important person: YOU.

These books will allow you to leave notes, and with them, there will be highlighters if you get the book. You will often revisit these tools, using them to grow from turbulence to survival and, eventually, to overcoming. This is the goal, and you hold the key inside you.

This is dedicated to my children in hopes they never forget that anything is possible and life is worth living, no matter how turbulent it gets.

I..Love..You more than you will ever know.

I am thankful for my life and the ability to see life the way I do. I am thankful for most things in my life and lessons learned, and I hope this book helps you all get to that place in life, also.

I understand all of this is repetitive, please understand I learned there is more than one way to do all things so, it may seem mundane, but together we can find one of them to work for you. If you have heard this before or tried this before, I'm gonna say try it again in a different way. Because it works as long as you actively do it and allow the spirit to be felt and heard.

You Got This. Do not give up on the most important thing in this world. Yes, I'm talking about you!!

Table of Contents

Page Left Blank Intentionally

CHAPTER 1

Start Someplace

Some days can feel like Groundhog Day, numb, yet consistent, filled with the safety of knowing exactly how the day will unfold. There's comfort in this predictability, but the truth is, comfort doesn't necessarily mean success. Other days, it feels like a struggle, emotions run high, expectations weigh heavy, and past experiences hinder the drive for life, leaving little room for new possibilities.

Change often feels overwhelming, and sometimes, we struggle to understand that life is worth living. But living is about learning. It's about making mistakes and growing from them. Someone once asked me to teach them everything I've learned in life, and I was taken aback by the question. How could I even explain all the lessons I've learned? There have been countless lessons, but at the core of it all, one thing stands true, they are mine to learn, and mine to avoid repeating.

I remember being a young child, feeling deep down that life must have more to offer. At that time, I didn't know what that "more" was or what it would look like, but the thought stayed with me. Now, in my late 40s, I finally understand what that feeling meant. I've learned how to start over every day. There were times when my worst day felt like it would never end, and all I could hope for was to fall asleep, just so I could begin again the next day.

Start right now. Yes, right now, as you read this sentence. Close the book, set it down, and shift everything in your mind to what the spirit is asking for: strength, dedication, and power.

Tomorrow morning, as you wake and take your first breath, pause for a moment. Pay attention and simply say, "Thank you." Don't tie it to anything specific—just feel it. Then, as you place your feet on the ground, say it again. As you stand up, say it once more.

This small act of gratitude is easy to give. The more we practice saying "thank you" for the little things, the easier it becomes to give thanks for the big ones.

So, listen up: "Thank you." Yes, I'm talking to you. With grace and gratitude, now it's your turn. Say it out loud. Hear yourself. Walk around and say it again: "Thank you." This is the beginning. This is the start.

Am I being redundant? Yes, I am because the real change requires repetition. To build something meaningful, we must do it over and over again. And saying "thank you" is far easier than saying "I'm sorry" and truly meaning it.

How ready you are to change depends on how deeply you're willing to live in a space of gratitude. Here's a practice that worked for me: I took a black marker and wrote "Thank you" on all my mirrors, yes, all of them. (Don't worry, it comes off with a little Dawn dish soap!)

When people use my bathroom, they often ask, "Why do you have 'thank you' written all over the mirror?" I simply replied, "Did you read it?" Most of the time, they say yes. Then I ask, "How did it make you feel?"

Usually, they'll shrug and say something like, "Funny" or "Nice," though they don't always know why. And I tell them, "That's all I wanted, for you to allow yourself to feel good."

Gratitude is powerful. It has a way of turning ordinary moments into extraordinary ones. So start now. Let it be simple. Let it be consistent. And above all, keep it sincere. Thank you.

Start with one breath, one step, one day at a time, beginning with "Thank you." See how it feels. Slowly, incorporate a journal into your practice. Before you know it, gratitude will become second nature—something you express even while driving home, as if your mind is actively seeking things to be thankful for.

Eventually, your subconscious will take over, gently reminding you: "Thank you."

This practice creates a moment of peace between Me, Myself, and I. A much-needed space for grace and gratitude. Starting with "Thank you" nurtures self-compassion and fosters an understanding of your own needs. It opens your eyes to the countless things in life to be grateful for.

If you've embraced this practice of gratitude, you might now be asking, What's next?

Starting somewhere is never just about taking one step. To reach your destination, you need multiple steps, approached with patience and focus. So let's take the next step: "I'm sorry."

What does "I'm sorry" really mean? How often do we misuse it?

We say, "I'm sorry" for things we aren't responsible for or don't truly regret, like apologizing for how someone feels or for situations beyond our control. Sometimes, we may even say, "I'm sorry" when what we truly mean is, "I feel compassion for you."

Let's return to the root meaning of "sorry." According to the dictionary:

"To be sorry is to feel regret or sadness, especially about something you did."

If we express regret for things that aren't our fault, can we replace "I'm sorry" with silent understanding or compassionate words instead?

For self-love, growth, and empowerment, it's also vital to learn how to say, "I'm sorry" to yourself. This is not about guilt or shame, it's about forgiveness, hope, and love.

Saying "I'm sorry" to yourself can be a way to start over, to let go of regrets and embrace your humanity. It's not the same as apologizing for a tragic loss or expressing sorrow for someone else's pain. Instead, it's a practice of empathy for yourself.

Ask yourself: When was the last time you gave yourself the same grace you extend to others?

This step is for you, to forgive yourself, to understand your own struggles, and to acknowledge your imperfections. This is the kind of empathy that leads to self-control, self-compassion, and the realization that you are the creator of your own life.

Take a breath. Take a step. Let "Thank you" and "I'm sorry" guide you toward deeper self-awareness and empowerment.

As we explore the meaning behind "I'm sorry," take a moment to say it to yourself: "I am sorry." What does it feel like? Can you feel it in your body? Is there pressure, discomfort, or numbness? Whatever arises is okay.

Now, let your mind rest. Focus on your body and how you feel. Then, say it again: "I am sorry." Without labeling the feeling, simply observe what's there. This is the first step in tuning into your emotions without judgment.

Over time, I've learned to take this a step further by refusing to let my mind immediately label every emotion I experience. For example, if I wake up with pressure in my chest, my mind might label it as "anxiety" or "unease." But now, I have stopped it. Instead of naming the feeling, I give myself space to just simply feel it.

Your subconscious is already working through questions like: *Do I want to keep this feeling? Can I release it?*

So, what if we simply focus on saying "Thank you" more often? Over time, this practice will shift how you experience emotions. When something positive happens, your first instinct will be to express gratitude. Soon, this habit will fuel a sense of power and control. You'll feel a surge within your chest as you embrace both strength and grace.

Starting with Gratitude

The first step in transformation is simple: "Thank you."

This may seem small, but it's profound. Write "thank you" on your mirror, make it your screensaver, place it in your workspace, or keep it somewhere you will see every day. At first, it may feel awkward or even pointless, but trust me, the impact is real. Gratitude is the starting point for change.

Surviving vs. Overcoming

To survive often means to cope. But coping is just about getting through the day. It keeps you standing, but it doesn't help you move forward. Overcoming, on the other hand, is about taking control, living intentionally, and moving forward with purpose.

I remember the moment when I made a decision once: Mind, body, and spirit came together when I said, "Stop merely coping—learn to live and overcome." This was about embracing my life with grace and gratitude as the foundation.

- Thank you for knowing.

- Thank you for learning.

- Thank you for allowing self-love and growth.

When we survive, we often develop unhealthy coping mechanisms. But when we choose to change, we can thank those struggles for the lessons they brought us, even if those lessons came through pain.

Gratitude for the Lessons

It might be uncomfortable to give thanks for the difficult parts of your journey, but remember: Every challenge carries a lesson. By acknowledging these lessons, you take back control.

Trauma—whether physical, emotional, or mental, shouldn't be overlooked or brushed aside. I'm not suggesting you to forgive others or dismiss the harm caused. But I am encouraging you to thank the experience for the growth it allowed.

- Thank you for teaching me what to watch for.

- Thank you for helping me choose a different path.

- Thank you for strengthening my resilience.

Moving Forward

Ask yourself:

- What was the lesson in this experience?

- How did it make me feel?

- Do I want to continue feeling this way?

If the answer is no, then you have the power to move forward. Healing starts when you choose it, and gratitude is the key to unlocking that transformation.

Gratitude isn't just for the good times, it's for recognizing the lessons that even hardships offer. It's about creating a life filled with growth, love, and empowerment.

Stronger, Brighter, and Ready for the Next Level

The fire inside you burns brighter, guiding you toward the next level of your life. You've begun your journey with gratitude, saying, "Thank you, thank you, thank you." This is just the beginning, a jump start. But now, we come to a deeper, more complex part of the process: "I'm sorry."

For many of us who've experienced damage and lost self-worth, we start apologizing for everything, just to keep the peace and to avoid conflict. But what does "I'm sorry" really mean?

We've spent time walking around saying thank you, but now are we supposed to apologize for it? NO!

Saying "I'm sorry" means empathy, feeling regret or sorrow about something. But do you truly feel bad for everything you apologize for? Do you feel bad when someone doesn't hold the door for you? Do you feel bad when someone leaves the lights on or takes up space that isn't theirs?

The truth is, you don't. What happens is that when we don't value ourselves, we carry the burdens of others, taking on their yuck to fill the emptiness within. We tell ourselves we have to carry these burdens because we can, because we believe it's what we're worth.

This mindset had to change for me, and it must change for you, too. Start with thank you, then move to I'm sorry, but only for things that truly deserve regret, not for the unnecessary burdens others place on you.

Understanding "I'm Sorry"

The phrase "I'm sorry" has a deeper meaning, divinely given to us. But over time, we've misused and abused its true power. This has dulled our spirits, making us think we must carry the weight of the world on our shoulders.

When we bargain between thankfulness and an apology, our spirit starts to fill with strength. But that strength comes from learning not to apologize for things that are simply beyond our control.

Do not take on someone else's rocks. If someone walks into a space they shouldn't, that's their responsibility, not yours. You don't need to apologize for their actions. You don't have to shrink yourself to make others comfortable.

Simplifying Life: The Four Key Phrases

You, as a person of mind, body, and spirit, are simple yet complex. Four simple phrases can empower and improve your life every day:

1. Thank you
2. I'm sorry
3. Please forgive me
4. I love you

If you're already practicing these, I'm sure, it might feel unfamiliar or even a little awkward. That's okay. Stick with it. Say thank you for the emotions and feelings you're experiencing, and say I'm sorry for not fully understanding the depth of these phrases before.

Moving Into Forgiveness

Now let's talk about "Please forgive me." What's the difference between saying "I'm sorry" and asking for forgiveness? Many of us want to skip this part because it feels like too much effort, but it's necessary. What does forgiveness mean, and who are we asking to forgive us?

Here's the truth: You didn't make yourself feel this way.

You didn't choose the pain, the hurt, or the emotions you carry. But let's pause for a moment, and I'll explain.

If your heart is full, whether with hate or love, it still carries weight. That weight hurts, and we must work to change it. Forgiveness isn't about pretending the hurt didn't happen, it's about lightening the load. It's choosing to heal what you didn't cause, so you can stop reliving what broke you.

The Power of Transformation: Embracing Change

As we continue this journey, remember that real change doesn't always happen instantly. The feeling and power of transformation may not change immediately, but by taking small, intentional steps, you will gradually notice the difference.

Start with just saying it, say the words to yourself, either in your mind, in the mirror, or aloud. Allow any feelings that surface to emerge, even if they feel uncomfortable. I promise, this discomfort will eventually lead to something deeply rewarding.

You're not alone in this. The intention to change often comes with fear about following through, and while I can't guarantee the exact outcome, I do know that over time, you will see results.

Breaking It Down: "Please Forgive Me"

Let's dive deeper. The phrase "Please forgive me" can be transformative. It's an invitation to speak with empathy and love, but it starts with grace for yourself. It all begins with how we speak to ourselves and the reality we create in the present.

If you've been holding onto thoughts or memories of past experiences, this is the best way to begin to take control. Yes, overcoming means controlling. What do I mean by control? You control what consumes your thoughts, emotions, and feelings. When you allow something or someone to dominate your mental and emotional space, you lose control. But when you make the conscious decision to control who affects you, when they affect you, and how much energy you allow them to take, you reclaim that power.

This is where thank you and I'm sorry come into play. We often forget we have this control because we don't exercise it. But with practice, we begin to give ourselves the support and grace needed to strengthen our spirit and direct our lives.

Repeating the Process

Begin by slowly repeating these two phrases to yourself, first in your mind, then aloud when you're ready. Why repeat them? Because Me, Myself, and I are always listening. Your words matter, they shape your reality. Healing and overcoming take time, and it's perfectly fine to go at your own pace.

Halfway There: Commit to Yourself

Now, let's pause and reflect. Remember, this is just the beginning. These steps are tools to help you on your healing journey, and the true change happens when you commit to yourself, not for anyone else. You can only put the right tools in place for your success when you decide you are worth it. So, buckle up, there's more to come. It will all lead you toward the life you were meant to create.

The Power of Self-Forgiveness

The phrase "Please forgive me" is powerful. Why forgive yourself? Because you didn't cause your pain. If life's tragedies or other circumstances happened to you, I understand. But the healing begins with letting go of the energy you've spent holding onto those experiences. You need to forgive yourself for overthinking, for holding onto things that are no longer serving you, and for letting them block your progress. Yes, it's hard to hear, but the truth is: You must forgive yourself to heal. This process allows you to empty out the emotional energy that's been wasted on things beyond your control and begin the work of moving forward.

Embracing the Pain and Moving Forward

Forgiveness might feel like you're begging, but it's not. It's a form of acceptance, of loving and accepting yourself. This is where grace comes in: giving yourself the ability to be heard, loved, and accepted. When you allow this acceptance, you create safety, courage, and inner strength, which ultimately help you overcome obstacles and create a path for growth. The most important person in this process is YOU!

Saying "Please forgive me" out loud gives you the space to release whatever emotions are holding you back. Cry if you need to; it's all part of the healing process. Your tears are a release, making room for love, growth, and joy to come in.

The Power of Commitment and Truth

Now, let's talk about commitment. When you say you can't, I want you to stop and ask yourself: Am I able, or do I simply not want to? The word "can't" carries a sense of uncertainty. You need to commit to yourself. Believe that you are capable and worthy of all good things, and that you can create the change you need.

The commitment to yourself is everything. Consistency in practicing gratitude, forgiveness, and love will change your life in ways you can't yet imagine. Over time, these small steps will accumulate, and soon they'll feel monumental.

The Final Step: I Love You

Now, let's reach the final and most important step: I Love You. Yes, I do, even though I don't know you, I love you. But now, it's time for you to love yourself. I know it may feel strange at first, but listen closely: You've been showing yourself love all along, you just haven't acknowledged it yet. You've protected yourself, even when you didn't recognize it. Now, it's time to give yourself the love and grace you deserve.

When you say "I love you", it might feel awkward or even painful. But remember, pain can also be a sign of healing. When you're full of emotion, whether joy or pain, your body experiences physical sensations. So, when you feel pain from saying "I love you", it's just your body's response to something new and healing. Trust that the discomfort is part of the process.

Trusting Yourself

I'm asking you to trust yourself now more than ever before. Trust yourself both consciously and subconsciously. I know the negative thoughts you've carried throughout your life. So now, I'm asking you to tell your mind to stop. Then, say "I love you" over and over, even if it feels uncomfortable. You may cry, but remember that crying releases what needs to be let go of, creating space for love and growth.

Making Room for Healing

By repeating the words "I love you," you begin to embrace true forgiveness. It's not about the other person; it's about you, the most important person. You've been with yourself all along, through every moment, and now it's time to acknowledge the love and care you've always had for yourself, even if you didn't recognize it before.

This process helps you forgive even the smallest lies you've told yourself, like when you pretended to like something you didn't, just to fit in. It also helps you forgive the larger traumas, allowing you to make room for the joy, hope, and love you deserve.

Remember, you are a unique and beautiful part of the mosaic of life. Your edges, your curves, your colors, your brilliance, they are all yours. Let your light shine, because you are worthy of everything beautiful life has to offer.

_____

_____

_____

_____

Reflection Time

Below, take some time to reflect on what you've felt and learned from this chapter:

_____

_____

_____

_____

CHAPTER 2

MAKE UP YOUR MIND

If you're jumping right into this, you may feel like you've already done so much. And you have! But we're not done yet. It is the true beginning. Something in this book will stay with you for the rest of your life. So let's explore your choices, work through them, and find what will truly stick. In the previous chapter, I used the Ho'oponopono consciously and subconsciously. It's about understanding its components and reintroducing yourself to what's been given to you: *I'm sorry, please forgive me, thank you, and I love you.*

All of this is done out of love—rediscovering yourself and realizing that it's more than okay to love yourself. This is the step where you "make up your mind" regarding your mind. It's a skill of its own, a tool that can regulate your emotions, feelings, and perspectives, helping you understand how and when to deal with situations, how to react, and how to move forward. It's so powerful. Teaching yourself to shift from negative thought patterns to positive ones can be difficult, depending on your surroundings, habits, willingness, and openness to change. It requires grace for yourself when it's not easy.

A trauma response is hard to control because it was put in place to protect you. When something looks, sounds, smells, or feels like a situation from your past, your brain may trigger a protective reaction. In those moments, I'm going to ask you to first breathe. Take a step back and ask, "Is this the same situation?" One of the easiest ways to ground yourself is by using the 5-4-3-2-1 method:

- Find 5 things you see.

- Find 4 things you hear.

- Name 3 things you feel.

- Name 2 things you smell.

- Finally, bring your awareness back to yourself, the one in the present space.

Now, ask yourself how you would like the outcome to unfold and how you'd like to respond, given that you've learned a lesson and survived. As you begin to take control of the hope you desire, you'll slowly gain the strength to respond differently and learn new ways to prevent an outcome you don't want.

Changing your mind begins in your mind. The mind is a massive muscle, constantly communicating with the body and spirit. Memory and recall are connected to your intuition, but sometimes your intuition gets shoved aside. Yes, you do have control over your mind. If a traumatic memory or a repeated reaction plays over and over in your head, how do you stop it? The answer is surprisingly simple:

Yell *"Stop! Stop! Stop!"* or *"No! No! No!"* out loud.

I can recall many moments when I replayed memories from my past in my head. I would hear my mother's voice, telling me I ruined her weekend, or calling me worthless, over and over. Eventually, I started yelling at myself to stop: *"Stop! Stop! Stop!"* or *"No! No! No!"* until the thought would cease. It was frustrating and difficult at first. I was afraid of what others might think, and uncomfortable with the physical and mental sensations of doing this. I wondered: "Am I lying to myself? Am I being authentic?"

But the truth is, by allowing those negative thoughts to overcome me, I was denying my truth. My truth was that I deserve peace, love, and joy within my balance. That's the focus—continuing to overcome and keep your attention on living to live.

Now, ask yourself: What do you want? Do you want frustration and fear? I'm not saying this judgmentally, but ask yourself if that's really how you want to live. Do you even know what it feels like to experience balance, joy, and love? I didn't. And it was hard for me to say yes to those things because I had never known them. I had to push myself out of my comfort zone to experience it. This process allowed me to make a decision about what I truly wanted.

Here's a saying I use with some of my clients: *How do you know if you like peanut butter?* It takes a big commitment to try it, not knowing if you'll react to it good or bad, but you still choose to experience it to find out. That's what you need to do in your healing. Make the choice to experience it and be ready for the outcome. That way, you can decide if you like it or not, and stick to being authentic to yourself and your truth in the decision you made.

In this process, make a choice, stand by it, and hold true to your answer. That doesn't mean you can't change your mind later—this is the beauty of loving yourself. It gives you the allowance to try new things, create the life you want, and change course as needed. The time and space you have now are not defined by your past but by your current mindset and your decision to change.

Hey, by the way, I still love YOU!

Take a deep breath, and let's keep going. The hard part is recognizing that it takes 21 days to form a habit. But did we consider what we need to give up to make room for this next part? This process isn't just a "must," it's the foundation to start.

Oftentimes, we or others ask, "Why change? Why now?" Much like in building a home, you need a solid foundation. But most of the time, we forget the step of sourcing, finding the right surroundings, and deciding what we want in our lives before laying that foundation.

So, *why change?* First, because you are worth it. Second, give me a good reason why not.

I'm going to ask you to decide what you are changing before you decide why. Step one is realizing what you truly need. A *need* is something essential for survival; a *want* is a desire you can live without. We'll dive deeper into desires later, but first, you need to define your needs.

Often, I ask people to make a list like this:

- I need food.

Now, dig a little deeper—what types of food do you need? Be specific, yogurt, turkey burgers, etc. The more time you spend reflecting, the more honest you are with yourself, the better. It took time for you to get here, and it will take time for you to evolve into the new, growing version of yourself.

Once you've made a list of your needs in depth, you can identify what you already have and what's missing. These gaps represent the areas you need to change. Once you've identified these, you can start writing your "why." Why do you need these things?

At this stage, we've explored the surroundings of your pre-built life. Only now are you ready to write your *why* and begin working on your foundation. Before you lay the concrete, you need to map out the electrical systems, plumbing, and structure. This is your vision, seeing yourself with everything you need and deserve.

This is why I encourage you to write in a notebook, adding to it as you go. Watch how your list of needs transforms into a list of *haves*.

Yes, you can't keep a need in the "need" section forever. At some point, you need to move it to the *have* section, where you can say, *"I have..."* This shift acknowledges what you've worked for, showing grace and gratitude for your efforts. It's essential to take time to appreciate yourself. By doing this, you allow yourself to move forward without clinging to something you no longer need, and this will become part of your goal-setting process.

The mind is often a misunderstood space, one in which we only use a small portion. So why not continue to learn and grow, allowing it to also take a back seat in the mind-body-spirit journey? In this chapter, we have learned strategies to help retrain the mind—maybe even fool it until you gain the strength and confidence to increase your courage and become stronger than you were yesterday.

The mind is a place of influence, programming, and intellect. From a very young age, we learn concepts like hot and cold, good and bad, rules and regulations, emotions, and behaviors. Much of this learning happens simply by observing those around us and internalizing their feelings about different situations. Let me give you an example:

If your mom holds you close, rocking you in a chair until you fall asleep, you've learned feelings of security, love, safety, peace, and joy. On the other hand, if you're placed in a crib to fall asleep on your own, you might feel abandonment, fear, being stuck, or a survival instinct at a very young age. This is not about blaming anyone for what happened in the past—there's no going back to fix or change it, but it's about creating awareness of everything you've learned from your environment.

So, let's bring in the Ho'oponopono practice—*I'm sorry, please forgive me, thank you, and I love you*—to release the negative aspects of this early learning and allow the brain to be retrained with appreciation for the lessons learned.

The hard part is realizing that some of the habits we developed during childhood—often out of a need to survive—might have shaped how we love ourselves and others, as well as how we value what we deserve and should receive. Now, remember, we're focusing on thoughts right now. By allowing the brain to step aside or be retrained, we can create balance and understanding, giving room for growth in other areas of our brain.

The brain listens to us, so when we speak, our words can shift and change the direction of our thoughts and the cycles we experience. If you've completed the exercise above and identified what you need and what you lack, you'll start to see some of the shifts needed to overcome fears, traumas, or old mental programming. What do I mean by this?

Well, when we focus on what we need and start speaking about it, our negative thought patterns related to those needs can begin to shift. Unfortunately, we may also justify why we should keep thinking in those ways, thinking that *this* is part of the healing process. Truthfully, it's not.

Let me give you an example of how this works. For instance, let's say *I, Tina, need communication with my spouse*. Now, if I follow the regimen, I'll write down why I need this. Here's an example:

"I feed off of learning and having great conversations about subjects I know and don't know. It helps me feel smart and helpful, and gives me the opportunity to learn new perspectives and approaches. At times, this can be more attractive to me than someone's eyes (though I really like eyes). To help my mind, body, and spirit feel nourished by my partner, I need to hear feedback and opinions from them. To me, it shows love, authenticity, and vulnerability, which in turn shows that I have their grace, trust, and support. I need this in a partnership to settle my desire for excitement."

You can go as deep as you'd like with this. In doing so, remember to reflect on what happens when you don't receive what you need. This reminder helps reinforce the importance of not settling or sacrificing your values and needs. Speaking about your needs helps your mind see their value and empowers your body to feel the excitement you get when those needs are met.

As you can see, this process can get quite deep, and that's okay. The more you allow yourself to be seen, the better. Allow yourself to be seen. But once the need has been fulfilled, be sure to move it to the "have" section. For example: *I, Tina, have communication with my partner.*

You have the power to change your mind and feed what is needed, rather than depending on what you were shown as you grew up. As we work more on body and spirit, you'll see the strength that these practices bring. When your mind, body, and spirit work together, they become like a three-legged table of your life that will be strong enough to bear the weight of the world's challenges, while creating the beauty you desire.

I _____ Need _____

I _____ Need _____

I _____ Need _____

I _____ Need _____

I _____ Want _____

I _____ Want _____

I _____ Want _____

Why do I need and or want these things?

_____

_____

_____

_____

_____

_____

_____

_____

_____

_____

_____

_____

_____

Build a Relationship With You

What exactly is Tina talking about? Let me break it down for you.

First, decide to make a promise to yourself. This promise is like the ones you make to your best friend—to always love and be there for them, or a promise like, "I'll give you candy if you finish the dishes." These promises are easy to break and unreliable. So, how do you determine your level of commitment to yourself when you decide to do the work?

By now, I hope you're feeling stronger in your honesty, and your mindset has shifted to a more positive place, allowing you to truly believe that the change you seek is possible—for you! This change is yours to own, and with it, you can embrace all the wonders of seeing yourself in a new light.

In this chapter, you'll learn to "date" yourself. You'll use the tools you've been introduced to and discover more about your needs and wants through balanced activities and self-reflection. This process will help you uncover your "why" and "what." It's essential to learn how to apologize, express gratitude, feel remorse, and love yourself in a way you might only have seen in movies or read about in books.

One of the most well-known promises is marriage, but in today's world, divorce is often seen as an option. While divorce may be necessary in some cases, other times relationships can be saved by understanding each other's needs and wants. Yes, this may seem repetitive, but that's the point, it needs to stick. A strong promise has the power to help you thrive, not just survive by coping.

As you go through this process, you'll continue to learn more about yourself. There are countless tools, like the 5 Love Languages and self-assessment tests, that can provide guidance based on your answers. But ultimately, the answers you seek are already within you.

Your thought process, emotions, and reality will guide how you answer these deep questions about what you need, desire, and deserve. It's important to give yourself the time and space necessary to go through each step so that when you begin this promised journey, you can be honest, truthful, and courageous in discovering what you're truly willing to do. This will allow you to make a sincere promise to yourself, rooted in hope, faith, and love.

A promise is a verbal contract—similar to the way a handshake was seen as binding in the past. Today, you don't see handshakes as often, especially after COVID, but making eye contact and using clear, concise words can have the same effect. In making a promise to yourself, it's important to create reminders that will keep you accountable. In this chapter, I'll share a few techniques to help you along the way.

One method often suggested by teachers is journaling. However, did you know that some of the things you write in your journal should be burned? This is a symbolic way of letting go of what no longer serves you, creating space for your new commitment to yourself.

Personally, I like to use a black Sharpie (don't worry, Dawn dish soap and a little elbow grease will remove it) to write on the mirrors in my home. I have four key phrases on each one: "I'm sorry," "Thank you," "Please forgive me," and "I love you." These words serve as daily reminders of what I need. On my children's mirrors, I add affirmations to support them, like "The body keeps score" and mantras that help them shift their mindset when they say something like, "My knee hurts" or "My hand hurts." A positive affirmation can help reframe their thinking.

Did you know one of the most powerful times to change your mindset is while you sleep? The subconscious mind is especially receptive during this time, making it the perfect moment to start working on lasting transformation.

Meditation and manifestation are powerful tools for healing, and using certain sound frequencies—such as ketones—can help enhance your journey. You can find these types of music or guided meditations on YouTube. Listening to them can make your sleep more efficient and productive, which in turn can accelerate your healing process. However, note that to create a lasting habit, you'll need to listen regularly, ideally for about 30 days. Change doesn't happen overnight, and it's through repetition that the subconscious begins to shift.

After my husband passed away, I would listen to these meditations, but I struggled with falling asleep. Every day, I hoped I would wake up from the nightmare and that everything would be fine. If you find yourself unable to sleep after trying a meditation three times, try switching the tone or words to something that resonates more deeply with you. Let your body guide you, allowing it to feel how the sounds and words affect you. Remember, your body "keeps the score"; it communicates with you in every moment you give it the lead.

When we make promises to ourselves, they can sometimes push us to act out of character or make us feel embarrassed. But that's okay. These promises are for you, so embrace the process and follow through.

When making a promise to yourself, it's essential to acknowledge both your spirit and body. They need to feel that you're considering them in your decisions. For example, let's talk about working out. Your mind might decide, "We'll work out today and for the next three days this week." If you haven't exercised in a while, your body may react to this new task with soreness or discomfort. If you push through without listening to your body, you risk injuring yourself. On the flip side, if you don't follow through at all, your body may feel neglected and rejected, holding onto that sense of abandonment.

That's why I recommend learning more about the concept of "the body keeping the score." Your body holds onto past and present experiences, and your future reactions will be shaped by the coping mechanisms you've developed over time. Understanding this can lead to deeper healing as you make promises to yourself with compassion and awareness of both your mind and body.

Let's return to the workout example. If by the second day of exercising, your body is so sore that it's difficult to move, this becomes a key moment. You could give up, which means your body would miss out on the activity it needs to stay healthy. Alternatively, you could push through the pain, hoping to get over the hump, but that could lead to injury, preventing future workouts. Lastly, you could listen to your body, rest, take vitamins or minerals, adjust your diet to aid recovery, skip a day, and resume the workout the next day. The key is to respect yourself, and that respect will extend to your body's needs.

Pay close attention, your body is always giving you signals, particularly when holding onto something negative. Staying hopeful and open will help ensure you are attuned to what your body is communicating.

Your body is unique, coming from your specific lineage. No one else is exactly like you, so take the time to understand it. We're just scratching the surface here with the idea of "the body keeping the score." You'll learn more about this concept in later chapters.

The Spirit's Need for Understanding and Acceptance

Just as your body needs care, your spirit requires understanding and acceptance. What does this mean? If you've been through challenges, turbulence, or trauma, your first instinct might be to protect your spirit— pushing it aside, hiding it to avoid further harm. But your spirit needs a voice. Giving it that voice means learning to love and trust yourself.

For example, imagine you trust a close friend with a secret. We all have secrets, after all. If that friend betrays you by sharing it or using it against you, your spirit may retreat, especially if it causes pain in your heart and body. However, you need to trust again, maybe not that same person, but you must find the courage to be vulnerable once more. Trust yourself to handle the aftermath of sharing parts of yourself with others, even though their reactions are beyond your control. You have control over how you respond and grow from the experience.

This process is crucial for healing both your body and spirit. Making a promise to your spirit is a significant step, carrying more power and meaning than you may initially realize. The spirit is the part of ourselves that we instinctively protect, often building defenses to ensure it remains unharmed. However, in doing so, we can silence the spirit, pushing it aside because vulnerability feels dangerous, leaving us open to potential pain.

But it's time to start engaging with your spirit again, allowing your inner voice to be heard. For true balance and fulfillment, we must create a safe space for our mind, body, and spirit to coexist harmoniously. When each is acknowledged and given a voice, it strengthens not only the spirit but also the body, allowing the goodness within you to emerge.

The promise you make to yourself now will positively impact all future relationships with others. The strength and communication you develop within your relationship with yourself will lay the foundation for growth, hope, and the faith that you truly deserve. You have the power to retrain your mind, relearn how to respond, and present your best, most authentic self to the world, if you allow yourself to.

Relationships teach us how to perceive our value and worth. The hope is that you come to see that you deserve all good things. When pain or hardship arises, having promised to love, protect, and respect yourself will enable you to release that pain more swiftly, with strength and courage. Using the words "I'm sorry," "Please forgive me," "Thank you," and "I love you" can help you navigate those moments. These words, though simple, have the power to guide you through letting go and learning the necessary lessons. Once you understand what it truly means to promise yourself love and respect, and once you experience how your mind, body, and spirit respond to it, there's no going back. You will no longer settle for relationships or circumstances that don't align with your values and the commitment you've made to yourself.

Reflection:

Think about your current relationship with yourself. Do you trust yourself? Have you made a promise to honor your body, mind, and spirit? Is it time to make a new commitment to yourself, one based on love, respect, and authenticity, a list of names of people you trust to hold you accountable.

_____

_____

_____

_____

_____

_____

_____

_____

I promise _____ I will _____ the next 30 days

to learn _____ and apply it to

_____

Daily Journal

Date _____

_____

_____

_____

_____

_____

_____

_____

_____

_____

_____

_____

_____

_____

_____

_____

_____

_____

I pick _____

as my accountability partner to help me overcome any fears I may have

during my promise to myself.

I will check in with them _____ for the next 30 days.

I will be honest with myself and them till I get stronger.

I give myself grace and gratitude every day as I learn this new promise to myself.

_____

_____

_____

_____

_____

_____

_____

_____

_____

_____

CHAPTER 3

Build a Relationship with Yourself

You might be asking, "I know myself, so why do I need to build a relationship with myself?" Well, have you ever truly been in a *relationship* with yourself? What does that mean? In this journey, we'll explore everything from getting to know yourself deeply to taking yourself on dates and truly embracing the best relationship you can have—with *you*. This will create an amazing bond and strength that will help you navigate life's turbulence.

Never did I think my best friend in the world would be me. I always felt I wasn't worthy of my own loyalty or my desire to protect myself. But little did I know, I've been doing this all along. Yes, I've been loyal to myself and protecting myself, though I never saw it as the right way at the time. Yet, I learned, grew, and changed from it. Let's dive into this together.

Did you know that less than one percent of people are willing to truly *do* the work to change? It's easy to talk about change, but true healing for long-term success comes from taking action. We are never done learning, we just have to choose whether we see the lesson or hold on to the negativity of the direction.

In this space, you need to be comfortable talking out loud to yourself, dating yourself, and realizing what you truly like or don't like. This chapter is about exploration, discovery, and challenges that you may have never experienced before. There is, however, a light at the end of the tunnel. As you begin this process, you'll start to see yourself treating yourself with so much grace and love that it will become second nature. You won't even have to think about it—it will just happen.

Your First Adventure: Small Missions

Your first adventure will involve small missions. You may need to repeat these if they feel difficult. These missions will look something like this:

- I'm sorry.

- Please forgive me.

- Thank you.

- I love you.

This is where you apply everything you've learned. Start with the following list:

What do you need?

_____

_____

_____

_____

_____

_____

_____

_____

_____

What do you like?

_____

_____

_____

_____

_____

What do you want?

_____

_____

_____

_____

_____

_____

What will you do again?

_____

_____

_____

_____

_____

It's important to take your time with this process. There's no rush, no time limit. Man-made time does not apply here. It took you time to get to this point, so let go of the pressure. I'm not here to hold you accountable, but you need to be ready to hold yourself to the changes you're making and the growth you're already experiencing.

Now that you've set up your individual journal, it's time to take yourself on dates. Yep, you heard me right!

The next time you're on your way home, stop and pick up something for yourself, whether it's a bouquet of flowers (if you like flowers), your favorite snack, or an item you've been wanting. This step must have a follow-through. Once you get home, ask yourself: Was this a need or a want? Why? How did it make you feel? Don't let your mind give you the answer, listen for the authentic truth from deep within.

Do this once or twice in the coming week, and document your feelings in depth. If you've never used an emotional wheel, I suggest looking one up online. If you feel sad, look deeper into the wheel to explore why. If you feel happy, do the same. Understanding your emotions is part of building a deeper relationship with yourself.

To truly commit to yourself, you need to be willing to give to yourself, receive from yourself, and discover what you really need or want. For example, if you've always wished for someone to buy you white roses and you finally buy them for yourself, notice how you feel when you receive them. Are you excited, or do you feel guilty? That's okay, let's dive into those feelings. When you walk through life with "me, myself, and I," giving and receiving from yourself, you will learn so much.

If you receive the white roses, place them in a vase, and realize you don't like them as much as you thought you would, that's part of the journey. Maybe you'll realize they're too easy to wilt, or maybe they just don't feel right. This process helps you discover what you truly want and need.

After 30 days of journaling and dating yourself, I recommend taking the Love Languages test. By then, you'll have a much clearer understanding of how to answer those questions. Additionally, taking a personality test would be valuable to see how you've evolved throughout this journey.

The best part of this process is that it's like going to school for relationships with yourself. When you start a new relationship, or if you're already in one, you'll engage differently. You'll be in your power, responding from an authentic self that is supported by a balanced mind, body, and spirit.

Now, make a list of the small gifts and dates you plan to give yourself over the next 30 days. These are your acts of self-love, and they will build the foundation for your relationship with yourself.

Write them down below:

_____

_____

(Here, you can include your list of planned dates and self-gifts.)

_____

_____

Remember, this is a journey of self-discovery and growth. Take your time, and enjoy the process. You're doing wonderful!

_____

_____

_____

_____

_____

_____

_____

_____

_____

_____

_____

_____

_____

CHAPTER 4

Surviving or Overcoming

As we work on ourselves or embark on a healing journey, we often hear phrases like, "I am a survivor" or "I survived this or that." Growing up, I always felt like something was missing, so I kept searching for what was next. Eventually, I realized that while I had survived up to that point, I didn't want to stay in survival mode. People often tell me to let go, move on, and move forward, but surviving and overcoming are two very different things, and accepting this distinction can be challenging.

Surviving means staying in the emotions, the feelings, and the space of what happened. How can that be truly letting go or moving on? It isn't.

Overcoming, on the other hand, is when you truly release the past and leave it behind. It's about no longer carrying the weight of those experiences but instead letting them remain in the past, so you can move forward with freedom.

Think of it in terms of cycles, like the cycle of life. Imagine a chain with links. If you keep removing links, the chain won't function the same way. Consider a bike chain: if you just remove links without replacing them, the cycle becomes shorter, not better. Instead of simply removing pieces, we need to add and replace links until we create a cycle that works best for us.

The challenging part is taking out a small link and adding a new one, it takes time, patience, and grace to allow the process. This is what overcoming looks like. My concept of surviving, however, is removing a link without replacing it and hoping the chain still works. Sometimes this may work temporarily, but ask yourself: how long will it last? Will I eventually need to take out another link and find myself stuck again?

Overcoming doesn't mean you're finished with the work; it just means you can move on to the next link or issue with more strength, power, and courage. When we survive, the link still remains part of the cycle. Some of these links, even if replaced, don't completely disappear, but they no longer dominate the cycle.

For example, when my husband passed away, the memory of that day played over and over in my mind, frame by frame, until his last breath, for almost a year. It's like a chain on a bike, if you take the time to label your cycle of life and address an issue or two, you can understand how this works.

If you look at the cycle of life, you'll see that it's driven by you. You can choose how fast or slow you go. But if you keep removing links without replacing them, you won't just face the problem of going in the wrong direction—you may end up not moving at all.

Take a moment and label a link you want to remove and replace.

The biggest challenge is knowing when the link is truly replaced. It's not always easy to know if the new link is working properly. So, it may take a couple of cycles to see how it fits. Breathe, it's okay, time is on your side. As you pedal your way through life, you can decide how fast you hit each section of the chain.

You are the biggest motivator here, and this is why this chapter is one of the last, it takes so much to get to this space in your healing journey. By now, you have developed helpful coping skills that sustain you in survival mode as you decide if you've truly overcome or if you need to make another change.

In my life, I've tried different links. Some took years to find, while others I knew immediately were the right fit. Please allow yourself the patience to find the right one to become an overcomer.

There are changes to be aware of when we shift from survivor to overcomer. Our surroundings and the people we keep company with will change. Do this with love, and remember that change often brings emotional discomfort, but most of the time, it's the kind of discomfort that leads to growth.

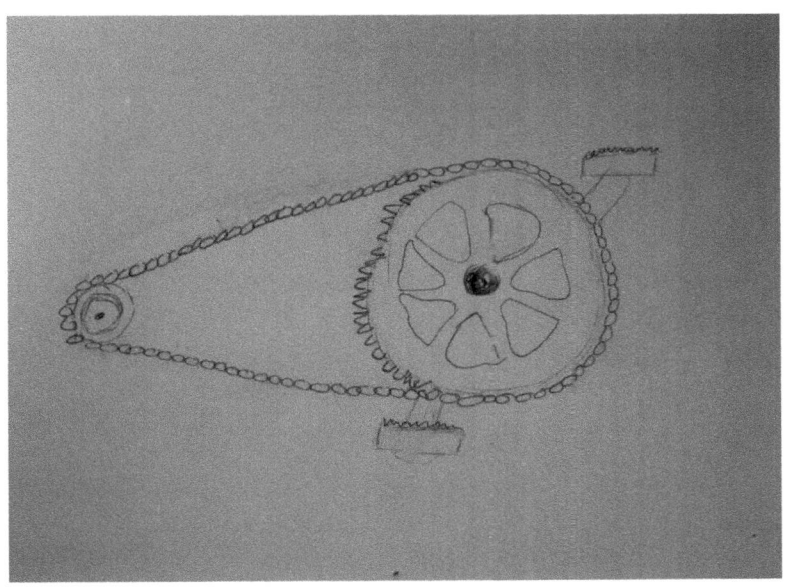

Yes, I drew this giggle with me a little.

There is something truly magical about aging. It's a richness that goes beyond the finest wine and far surpasses the fleeting allure of youthful freedom, where the world is your oyster. Aging brings a depth of meaning that youth can only dream of—a kind of wisdom gained through years of challenges, triumphs, and quiet moments of reflection. I've never been one to wish to go back and relive the past. Knowing what I know now, I wouldn't want to start over or do it all again. The life I've lived, the lessons I've learned, and the person I've become are all part of a journey I cherish deeply. These 50 years have shaped me in ways I couldn't have imagined, and instead of looking back, I feel a profound excitement about what's ahead.

The adventures waiting to unfold are limitless, whether it's exploring the beauty of the world, cherishing time with family, or continuing to grow emotionally and spiritually. Aging has gifted me with the ability to see each day as an opportunity to live fully, to appreciate the small miracles, and to embrace every breath with gratitude. It's a grace that couldn't have been fully appreciated in younger years but now fills life with purpose and meaning.

As you journey through life, it's essential to be patient and compassionate with yourself as you navigate change. Life's challenges often resemble a chain on a bike, with each link representing a connection to your past, your present, and your potential future. When a link becomes weak or no longer serves its purpose, it might feel necessary to remove it, but simply removing links without replacing them can leave the chain incomplete and unable to function.

Instead, consider this process as one of careful reconstruction. Allow the cycle to turn a few times after each adjustment before deciding to tweak it further. This gives you the time and space to adapt, reflect, and gain clarity. Change can be uncomfortable, even painful, but it is necessary for growth. Like the chain on a bike, the goal isn't quick fixes or shortcuts; it's about building a durable, functional system that allows you to move forward with confidence and purpose.

This isn't about assembling a quick-and-easy "build-a-bear" creation. It's about crafting something sturdy and reliable, where your power, choices, and actions become the driving force. Your effort propels the chain, ensuring forward momentum. The only way the chain stops is if you choose to stop pedaling, choosing stagnation or resignation instead of progress.

So, keep pedaling. Embrace the discomfort of growth, for it is through that effort that we discover new strength and resilience. The beauty of life lies not just in the destination but in the journey, the ride, the turns, and even the challenges that make us stronger. Aging isn't a loss; it's a gain, an unfolding of possibilities, and an opportunity to live with more grace, gratitude, and authenticity than ever before.

Take a moment to build your metaphorical chain. Think about the cycles you go through, whether in work, relationships, health, or self-discovery. Break these into categories, and consider which links in your chain are solid, which are weak, and which might need replacing. This exercise can help clarify where you are and how to move forward.

This space is also an excellent opportunity to explore the concept of the body keeping score. If you've read *The Body Keeps the Score* by Bessel van der Kolk, you know how deeply the body holds onto memories. If you haven't, don't worry. I'll touch on some key insights that might help.

Think about what it took to learn how to walk. What came first? Many people say crawling, but it's actually a process that begins with rolling, sitting, and then progressing to crawling and walking. Along the way, your body learned countless small lessons. How to put your hands out when you fall, how to duck when entering a small space. These were learned behaviors stored in the body's memory. Over time, the body began to perform these actions automatically, without conscious effort.

Now consider how the body also learns from negative experiences. For example, if you were hit in the face as a child, you may have learned to flinch. If this happened repeatedly, your body might have developed a state of constant readiness to protect itself. These physical responses can linger long after the danger has passed, creating patterns of fear and distrust. Over time, these patterns can influence not just your physical reactions but also your mindset, leading to a cycle of fear and limitation.

This is where you begin to relearn and create safety for your body and mind. The process of changing these deeply ingrained patterns requires patience and intentionality. It's about recognizing the links in your chain that are no longer serving you and replacing them with healthier, stronger ones.

For example, if you notice that fear is driving your decisions, you might pause and ask yourself what link in the chain is causing this reaction. Is it a memory? A belief? Once identified, you can start working on replacing that link with one that supports courage and trust. This process may take time and repeated effort, but with each adjustment, you're creating a cycle that works better for you.

As you date yourself, learning what you like, don't like, want, and need, you develop a clearer understanding of how to build a life that aligns with your values. This self-awareness allows you to apply new rules and boundaries to your life. As the cycle continues, you make changes one at a time, each one contributing to your growth and strengthening your courage and resilience.

Ultimately, the goal is to create a chain that moves smoothly, propelling you forward with clarity and purpose. By embracing this process, you cultivate a life filled with serenity, strength, and the ability to overcome whatever challenges come your way.

_____

_____

_____

_____

_____

_____

_____

Overcoming Survival and Sustaining Growth

Overcoming survival is a monumental step. It signifies resilience, perseverance, and the courage to face adversity. However, the journey doesn't end there. To truly thrive, you must learn how to sustain growth and navigate life's challenges. A key tool in this process is understanding and applying **boundaries**.

Boundaries are often misunderstood, yet they are vital for protecting your emotional, physical, and mental well-being. Let's start with their definition:

- *A boundary is a line that marks the limit of an area.*

- *It is also a limit of a subject or a sphere of activity.*

While these definitions describe boundaries as physical or conceptual, they can also be deeply personal and dynamic. Learning to identify, set, and maintain boundaries is essential for your growth and relationships.

Types of Boundaries

There are various types of boundaries, each serving a unique purpose in different areas of life:

1. **Time Boundaries:** These help you protect your time and manage how you allocate it.Example: Declining last-minute requests that interfere with scheduled priorities.

2. **Physical Boundaries**: These define your personal space and physical needs. Example: Expressing discomfort when someone invades your space.

3. **Conversational Boundaries:** These guide the topics you're comfortable discussing. Example: Politely steering conversations away from sensitive subjects.

4. **Relationship Boundaries:** These dictate the expectations and limits within your relationships. Example: Setting clear rules about mutual respect and communication.

5. **Content Boundaries:** These control the type of media, information, or interactions you expose yourself to.Example: Avoiding toxic social media accounts that affect your mental health.

6. **Emotional Boundaries:** These help protect your feelings and emotional energy. Example: Refusing to take on someone else's emotional burdens as your own.

Levels of Boundaries

Boundaries come in varying levels of firmness, much like road markings:

- **Soft Boundaries:**

Imagine a two-lane highway with a dotted line. You can cross it, only when it's safe. Soft boundaries offer flexibility but still require awareness and caution.

_____

- -

_____

- **Moderate Boundaries:**

Think of a double lane with solid lines. These lines caution you against crossing. While exceptions exist, they are rare and should be approached carefully.

_____

- -

_____

- **Hard Boundaries:**

Picture a concrete divider in the middle of the road. Crossing it is strictly prohibited and leads to serious consequences. Hard boundaries are non-negotiable and exist to protect you at all costs.

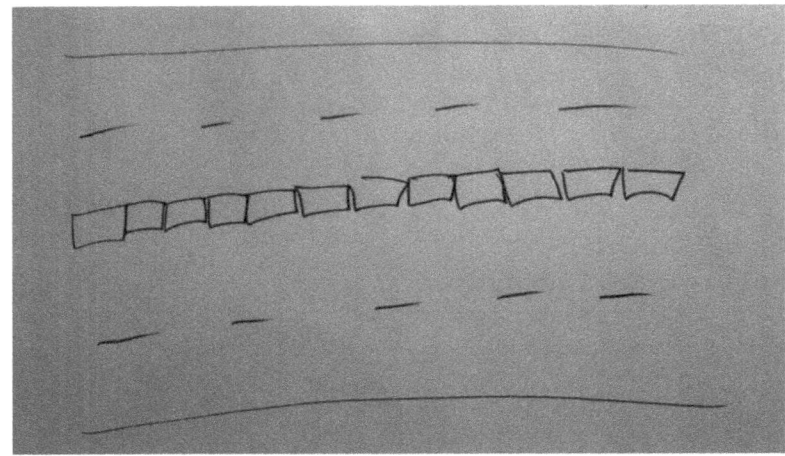

Understanding when to apply each level of boundary ensures you stay true to yourself and prevent others from imposing their will on you.

Take your time and work on your own boundaries: what are the absolute do not cross, and what (in some cases) are okay or acceptable.

Use the blocks above and fill in your hard boundaries, then ask yourself why is this your boundary, and what is the outcome you desire in doing.

The Growth Process

Every obstacle you overcome teaches you something new about yourself, your relationships, and the situation at hand. These lessons are the building blocks of personal growth and the foundation for healthy boundaries.

When you practice forgiveness and cultivate self-love, you gain clarity. You can better assess your boundaries, understand the dynamics of your relationships, and make decisions that prioritize your well-being.

Remember, growth isn't linear, and it takes time. Some lessons may not make sense immediately, but will become valuable later.

Building Your "Mary Poppins Bag"

Think of the tools and lessons you gather along the way as items in a "Mary Poppins bag." This isn't a heavy backpack you carry everywhere, but a bag you can set down and pick up as needed. Each experience— whether it teaches you resilience, courage, or patience—becomes a resource for future challenges. Over time, your collection of tools grows, allowing you to face life's uncertainties with confidence.

Embracing the Journey

The process of healing and growth can be turbulent. It requires patience, self-compassion, and a willingness to embrace the unknown. However, as you learn to set boundaries and protect your energy, you'll discover growth in self-love and courage.

Take it one step at a time. Trust that every effort you make, no matter how small, moves you closer to a healthier, more fulfilling life.

Now, let's talk about courage. Did you know there are seven types of courage? They include physical, social, moral, spiritual, emotional, intellectual, and creative courage. Each one plays a crucial role in our lives and needs to be nurtured and strengthened.

Although there are similarities among them, each type of courage serves a unique purpose. Together, they empower you to overcome challenges, maintain secure boundaries, and deepen your understanding of yourself.

Courage comes in many forms, each shaping our lives in profound ways.

Let's explore them:

Physical courage often resembles acts of heroism, like a firefighter running into a burning building. But it can also be as simple as leaving an uncomfortable or unsafe situation without saying a word. It involves taking physical action, training your body to react appropriately. Think of how we learned to walk, we stumbled, scraped our knees, and bumped our heads, but each fall taught us resilience.

Social courage empowers you to set boundaries and stand by them, no matter the social setting. It's about deciding where you go, who you interact with, and what you engage in, all while remaining true to your values. This courage allows you to maintain meaningful connections without compromising your integrity, whether by choosing to participate or opting out.

Moral courage is about standing up for your values, even when it's uncomfortable or unpopular. As you grow and reflect, you begin to understand what truly matters to you. Developing this courage makes it easier to break harmful patterns in relationships, work environments, or other areas of life. Teaching others how to treat you starts with honoring your own boundaries and staying true to what you believe in.

Spiritual courage can be the most challenging to develop because it requires faith in what we cannot see. Facing moments of embarrassment or pain strengthens your spirit, helping you trust in yourself and the process without relying on expectations. This courage teaches you to let go, embrace uncertainty, and find peace in

Emotional courage demands honesty. It's about acknowledging your feelings and understanding what truly makes you happy. Whether you dislike fish, love sunsets, or dream of living in the mountains, your preferences are valid. Pursuing what brings you peace may challenge some relationships, but those who truly matter will remain. Emotional courage shows your growth, allowing you to explore and address deeper emotions beyond surface-level anxiety.

Intellectual courage is highly personal. It's about learning to trust and celebrate your intellect. Paired with emotional awareness, this courage helps you offer yourself grace and recognize your achievements. It empowers you to move forward confidently, knowing you've invested in your growth and learning—not just for today, but for the future.

Creative courage brings joy and freedom. Seven years ago, I bought a home and embraced my love for color and design. I created a unique space with uneven wooden walls, bold blue and red paint, old barn wood above the mantel, and inspirational quotes on the stairs. I added a large chalkboard and replaced a window with double doors. Over time, I discovered my eclectic Spanish-inspired style, a reflection of my love for creativity and building a home that feels authentic for me and my children.

This is a lot to digest, so please remember in this section to give yourself grace and gratitude for all you do. Have tried and be excited for all you will do in the future.

Below is a small space to take some notes in this chapter because there is so much.

_____

_____

CHAPTER 5

Grace and Gratitude

As we wrap up this book, we've arrived at what I believe is the most important part of healing: grace and gratitude. Choosing to live life better than before isn't just about moving forward, it's about truly understanding forgiveness, reconnecting with yourself, and figuring out your needs and wants. Along the way, maybe you started dreaming again, setting goals to keep those dreams alive, and taking steps to make them a reality. You've also gathered tools to continue healing, set boundaries, and make meaningful changes.

Now, let's pause for a moment and say it together: THANK YOU. Yes, thank you to your mind, body, and spirit. Thank you for showing up for yourself.

But let's take a closer look, do you really know what grace means? Here's how it's defined:

- Simple elegance or a refined way of moving.

- Courteous goodwill.

- Doing honor or credit to someone or something simply by being present.

All these definitions beautifully align with living in peace and harmony—whatever that looks like for you. Grace is about slowing down, making intentional moves, and creating a life that feels authentic and fulfilling. It's not about rushing or competing. It's about honoring your own pace and journey.

Now, let's talk about courtesy. I'll admit, when I first dove into this, I had to look it up! Courtesy means being polite, respectful, and considerate. When you spent time reconnecting with yourself earlier in this journey, you probably uncovered your values, morals, and vision for the life you want to live. That's grace in action. It's about applying those principles to your daily life and giving yourself the same respect you offer others.

And here's a big one: giving honor to someone or something with your presence is also grace. That includes *you*. You deserve grace, even on the hard days, especially on the hard days. Life will challenge you, but grace gives you permission to move through those moments with compassion for yourself. Not because you just deserve it, but because you *owe* it to yourself.

Now, let's switch gears to gratitude. Grace and gratitude might feel similar, but they play different roles. Gratitude is about being thankful. It's about recognizing and appreciating the kindness you've received, whether it's from others or from yourself. Together, grace and gratitude create a powerful combination. They help you overcome obstacles, stay focused, and maintain peace, even in the face of challenges.

Gratitude reminds us to say "thank you" for every effort we make, no matter how small. It could be something as simple as getting out of bed or making your bed. Or maybe it's something big, like taking a bold step toward your dreams. Whatever it is, it matters. And just as others have been there for you unexpectedly, gratitude inspires you to give back when you can.

When you live with grace and gratitude, starting your day with peace becomes second nature. It might feel awkward at first, but over time, it becomes an intentional way of living. Grace helps you let go of what no longer serves you, while gratitude grounds you in the good. Together, they create a foundation for healing and growth.

But here's an important piece: you need to accept what you're giving to yourself. Grace and gratitude aren't just about giving, they're also about receiving. When your mind tries to replace grace with ego or gratitude with judgment, pause and refocus. You're in control. You can choose to shift your mindset and keep moving forward.

In my early 20s, I thought negativity and blame would bring me more help or attention. I spent years trying to follow the lessons I'm sharing now, and I wasn't always consistent. Sometimes, I stuck with them for six months, other times for a year. But life has a way of testing us.

I needed courage, courage to stay kind, to hold onto gratitude, and to react differently in hopes of seeing better outcomes. Recently, I heard an actress share that she wasn't raised with discipline or structure, and how hard it was to build those habits as an adult. She admitted to failing repeatedly, but she never quit.

I can relate to that. I wasn't taught how to live with grace or elegance, either. I've always been resourceful, unafraid to jump into challenges and figure things out. But there came a point when I realized I needed to love and respect *me*, not the version of myself I had trained to survive, but the woman I wanted to be.

Growing up, my grandparents and aunt on my mom's side, and my grandparents on my dad's side, showed me glimpses of grace, faith, and elegance. They planted seeds of hope that life could be more than what I knew.

By my 30s, I was a mother. I poured myself into my children, but I was so afraid of failing that I became a perfectionist. When things didn't go as planned, I'd spiral into frustration and self-loathing. While I loved my kids unconditionally, I neglected to extend that same love and grace to myself.

In trying to be everything for my family, I lost sight of myself. I wasn't showing my children the best version of me. Instead of modeling what they *should* do, I often demonstrated what they shouldn't. Looking back, I realize I lacked self-worth. I didn't see myself as a gift; I saw myself as someone to protect others and fulfill roles.

To truly lead and love my family, I had to start loving myself.

_____

_____

_____

_____

_____

_____

Final Thoughts

I share this because none of us are perfect. The gift of life is in the learning—in continually searching, creating, and finding what brings us peace and joy without guilt or imbalance. I've been blessed to learn from so many people. Their stories have shaped me, and I hope mine offers you something meaningful in return.

Wherever you are in life, start by acknowledging the gifts and wonders you already have, no matter how small. Gratitude grows from there. Perspective changes when you start small and build on it.

I hope this book helps you in some way. I've had books that changed my life and inspired me to keep reading, searching for the next one that would speak to my soul. The lessons I've learned, I carry like treasures, ready to share with my loved ones.

Remember, you are the conductor of your life. The courage and belief you cultivate within yourself will shine abundantly. I know I have so much more to share, but this is just a small start in hopes someone will have a moment of understanding the power you hold.

You are a perfect piece to this magnificent mosaic masterpiece called life. We need your color, shape, and size to help this world be as magical as it can be. And help support each other as we are being shaped.

THANK YOU!!!!!!!!!!

Resources

1. The Untethered Soul: The journey beyond yourself: By Michael A.

   Singer.

2. Ho'Oponopono: By Paul Jackson.

3. You can heal your life: By Louise Hays.

A Small Letter From Me To You

Hi, Hi, Hi!

Did you make your bed today?

Did you take a moment to give thanks?

Let's do it together now: take a big, deep breath in. Hold it for a count of five, then exhale gently through your lips like you're blowing a kiss. And now, say it: THANK YOU.

If you follow me on social media, you know this is how I love to start almost every day. It's a small ritual, but it's a powerful one.

This book is just the beginning of *The Turbulent Life* series, a foundation for so much more I hope to share with you. Life has so many twists, turns, and storms, and it's easy to lose sight of who we are or who we were meant to be. Sometimes, we never even get to discover that person. But here's the thing: give grace to your upbringing, to the circumstances that shaped you, and never stop moving forward. Survival is only the beginning; hope and transformation are waiting on the other side.

You are not alone. I don't claim to know everything, but I do know the incredible power of the mind, body, and spirit when we truly allow ourselves to discover them. Growth and change can feel uncomfortable, even scary, but I hope this book helps you find comfort in those moments and encourages you to keep going.

I've written this book for my Children first and foremost, for the people who've seen my journey up close and continue to inspire me every day. And I've written it for my friends, loved ones, and anyone who has witnessed the turbulence in my life and wondered how I found my way through. The answer is simple: self-discovery.

As a somatic coach, I've been privileged to practice and share these lessons with my clients. Together, we've explored these ideas, challenged old patterns, and embraced new beginnings. What I've written here is not just theory, it's lived experience, both mine and theirs. So as you walk this path, remember: you're never alone.

Thank you for trusting me enough to pick up this book and for being willing to start or continue your own journey. I'm honored to share this space with you, and I look forward to our next connection.

Love you so much,

Tina

NOTES